FROM
CRACK TO GARY

FROM
CRACK TO GARY

MY JOURNEY TO OUR SAVIOR, JESUS CHRIST

GARY THOMAS

iUniverse, Inc.
Bloomington

From Crack to Gary
My Journey to Our Savior, Jesus Christ

Copyright © 2012 by Gary Thomas.

All rights reserved. No part of this book may be used or reproduced by any means, graphic, electronic, or mechanical, including photocopying, recording, taping or by any information storage retrieval system without the written permission of the publisher except in the case of brief quotations embodied in critical articles and reviews.

iUniverse books may be ordered through booksellers or by contacting:

iUniverse
1663 Liberty Drive
Bloomington, IN 47403
www.iuniverse.com
1-800-Authors (1-800-288-4677)

Because of the dynamic nature of the Internet, any web addresses or links contained in this book may have changed since publication and may no longer be valid. The views expressed in this work are solely those of the author and do not necessarily reflect the views of the publisher, and the publisher hereby disclaims any responsibility for them.

Any people depicted in stock imagery provided by Thinkstock are models, and such images are being used for illustrative purposes only.
Certain stock imagery © Thinkstock.

ISBN: 978-1-4759-3609-4 (sc)
ISBN: 978-1-4759-3611-7 (hc)
ISBN: 978-1-4759-3610-0 (ebk)

Printed in the United States of America

iUniverse rev. date: 07/16/2012

To my Lord and Savior, Jesus Christ: I would not be here if it was not for your grace and mercy upon me.

To my parents, Henry Lee and Bessie Elizabeth Thomas: You are no longer on this earth, but I believe you are in heaven. I wish you were with me now to see the changes that I have made in my life. You are with me in spirit.

To all the readers who are struggling with addiction: There is a way out. Give your lives over to Jesus Christ. Once we surrender to him and profess that he died for all our sins and believe in him, the Father, and the Holy Spirit, our lives will no longer be the same. We will become new creatures in Christ Jesus, who will give us the strength to carry on. Believe in Jesus Christ—and he will set you free!

Introduction

This is to let you know how I was leading my life for the enemy (Satan). I was lying, cheating, and using all types of drugs that almost cost me my life. There was a day in my life when I was about to be killed. I called out the name Jesus, and my life was saved. I know there is power in the name of Jesus Christ. All we have to do is be open to making a change in our lives and be tired of being sick and tired. We need to turn over a new leaf in our lives so that we may possess and have the promises that God has given us for being obedient to his Word.

What you will gain from reading this book is how God will have his hands on your life even when you do not deserve to have him protecting you. Even though we are still breathing on this earth, God loves us. No matter what we are going through, a time will come when he will lift his grace and let the enemy devour you. It will be too late to live by his commandments because Satan has his hands on you. His only assignment is to kill, steal, and destroy you.

God was always in my life because of his grace and mercy. Even though I was going down a path of destruction, God made me realize that I could lead a better life by living my life for our Lord and Savior, Jesus Christ.

Chapter One

My Family

I was born in Ohio on May 23, 1959, to Henry Lee and Bessie Elizabeth Thomas. I was born in a project called the Kimmel Brook Homes on the east side of Youngstown. I am the youngest of nine children. My parents were born in the same hospital one day apart from each other. My dad's birthday was March 14, 1926, and my mom's was March 15, 1926.

I had five brothers and three sisters. Richard was born in 1944. Shirley was born in 1950. Allen (Buster) was born in 1951. Lana was born in 1952. William was born in 1953. Arthur was born in 1954. Larry was born in 1957. Denise (Neecee) was born in 1958. William died of pneumonia when he was an infant. As a kid, I remember we got everything that a kid should have.

My dad worked very hard to provide for us. He worked in the steel mills all of his life. He used to work sixteen hours a day to provide for us. I will not say that we were a perfect family. We were a dysfunctional family. I used to be very scared of my dad because he used to drink and come home and beat on my mother. I used to hide in my closet to get away from him. I remember my mother running away from him. He was abusive physically and mentally to her. I also had a stepbrother named after my father. I think my father realized what a good wife he had. As I got older, the fighting stopped.

All the neighborhood kids would come over to our apartment because we had everything. When I was about seven years old, all of us had gotten bikes. I told my dad that I knew how to ride a bike, but I did not. I really wanted to keep the bike. When I got on my bike, I was falling off of it everywhere. My dad had to go get training wheels. All the kids were laughing at me when I got training wheels, but that was something I was trying to avoid because of the embarrassment of having them. It did not take me long to learn.

My dad was a very hard worker. He provided for all of us. Some of us were a disappointment to him because he wanted his kids to be better than he was.

Chapter Two

Growing Up

When I was eight years old, I got my nickname. On a winter day, all the kids in the neighborhood were sliding on ice. As I was sliding down the hill right outside of our playground, I hit a dry spot. I fell and cracked my front tooth. I took off running to the house with my tooth in my hand. I was in major pain.

We used to make up a lot of games in the projects. The neighborhood kids would all be given nicknames. They started calling me "Crack Teeth." My neighbors were the Lampkins. One of their sons that we called "Jelly" gave me that nickname, and it stuck with me.

After about two years, my nickname went from "Crack Teeth" to "Crack" for short. Robert West was my best friend in the projects. He had a few nicknames that I did not agree with, so I came up with my own. I called him "Bobwob."

My dad was disappointed that some of his children did not graduate from high school. Richard did not graduate, but Shirley did. Buster, Lana, Arthur, Larry, and Neecee did not graduate either.

Lana used to run away from home a lot. She got in with the wrong crowd and started using drugs. I used to see her sniffing out of a paper bag a lot. I did not know what that was until later on. I found out that it was glue poured into a bag. Sometimes she would run away to other states. I still do not know how she was able to afford to go out of state like she did. I guess she had some people who were her enablers.

When I was about eleven years old, I started seeing a lot of things that people did. We had a good neighborhood. I will never forget Christmases. All the kids would come to our house because they knew that we would get a lot of toys.

My dad was the breadwinner in our house. My mom did not work unless it was voting time. She would work at the polls for that one day. My dad was great when it came to providing for his children.

Chapter Three

Moving out of the Projects

My dad always wanted the best for us, when I was thirteen; he had worked hard enough to move us out of the projects and into a house. In May of 1972, he moved us to a place on the east side called the Sharon Line.

Before we moved in, he did a lot of things to the inside and outside of the house. Our house was on Bott Avenue. He put in a finished basement with everything—including a wet bar. Larry and I helped him a lot by planting grass, trees, and shrubs. That was some hard work, but we did it gracefully, appreciating that we had were moving out of the hood.

Lana was still running away. In the new house, she would go out her bedroom window. She would still run away to different states. She got pregnant when I was about twelve years old. She had a son, Derrick Lamont Thomas. My mom came up with a nickname for him; she started calling him "Chico." She came up with the name because her favorite TV show was *Chico and the Man.*

Lana would run away and leave us—especially our mom—to take care of Chico. One time she ran away to Rochester, New York, and came back with a guy that looked like a pimp. We thought he was the father of her child. My dad did not take to this very well; he wanted no dealings with this man who was corrupting his daughter.

In the fall of 1973, she came back on some kind of drugs. She was talking out of her mind and we could not understand anything that she was saying. I was very scared. My dad did not know what to do and ended up calling Woodside Receiving Hospital. He asked them to come get her to see if they could figure out what was wrong. Woodside was a hospital where crazy people went to try to get better.

After two days, they called and said that she was still talking like she was crazy. On the third day, they called him to say that she had died from a brain tumor. This really shook me up because she would always take me places with her when she was not running the streets.

We had to make funeral arrangements for Lana. We never did find out what type of drugs took her away from us, and we could not get in touch with the pimp. We had lost a brother and a sister.

Chapter Four

Changing Schools

In our very small town, there used to be rival fights with people from the different sides of town. My sister and I did not want to change schools and get into fights. All we used to do was fight. Not many people used guns; at least we would live to see another day. When I got my first girlfriend, I started to use drugs and alcohol.

Neecee and I started going to our new school. We had a neighbor who was a traffic cop at a nearby school. We used to catch rides with him to East High School. We were supposed to go to North High School, but those schools used to fight all the time. We did not want to change schools and be confronted. I ended up hanging out with the wrong crowd. The school found out that we were supposed to go to North High. We ended up enrolling in that school.

Neecee went there for a while but ended up dropping out. I continued to go, and I tried to buy some friends. One of my friends from the projects and his family ended up moving around the corner from us. They called him "Bumstead" when he lived in the projects. He was a fighter too! We became really good friends then when they moved. We used to walk down to the Kimmel Brooks to see our old friends. At North High, he used to be my protector. Nobody messed with him because of his height and strength. He was my bodyguard.

I used to sneak liquor out of my dad's bar in the basement. I would replace it with water so that I could take it to school to buy some friends. I put it in pop bottles and hid it in my locker until recess. The people I wanted to be my friends would get drunk with the liquor I brought to school. I also used to skip school with my friends. We would go to my house for lunch and never go back. My dad was at work, but my mom would let me do this for some reason.

When my dad found out that I was smoking weed, he said, "Son, I know that you are smoking weed. I would rather you smoke it in the house instead of being out there in the streets smoking." I thought I had it going on. At fourteen years old, I was smoking weed in the house.

I made a lot of friends at North High. I got to know a lot of people. Some of my good friends were Tony, Del Rio, and Anthony. My first girlfriend was Mary. I was attracted one of her associates, Marlane. I left Mary alone. Marlane was the aunt of Tony and Anthony. At one time, they thought that I used them to get to her, but I did not. Mary was actually my first love. Marlane was a challenge for me, but I did have feelings for Mary.

Me, Tony and Anthony used to skip school and smoke weed on a pathway by the school. My skipping caught up with me several times. One time me and Del got in a car accident. He went through the windshield, but I only sustained a wound to my forehead.

As a junior Del, Tony, Anthony, and I went to Senior Day. We were drinking and smoking, but we got out of control. Tony and I got into a fight inside the car. Del stopped the car, but we continued to fight until we got tired. We made up right after that and continued to drink and smoke.

When we arrived at school, the principal, Lock P. Beachum, caught us and told us that he was holding us back a year. For some reason, I was the only one that was held back. I failed my freshmen year and my junior year. I was determined to graduate from high school to let my parents know that I could do it.

I was nineteen in the twelfth grade. I should have graduated in 1977, but I did not until 1979. I did it. My parents were proud of me because only two of their nine children graduated from high school. When I was beginning the twelfth grade, my dad set me down and said, "Son, I have been taking care of you for eighteen years. When you graduate, I want you to go out on your own."

Chapter Five

Leaving Home for the Military

When I graduated from high school, I enlisted in the Air Force. I enjoyed my time off after graduation by partying before I went to basic training in August. I went to Lackland Air Force Base in San Antonio, Texas, for eight weeks.

I was so homesick, but I did what I had to do to make it through. I was missing Marlane a lot. I couldn't wait for basic training to be over to go see my family and my girlfriend. In the beginning of October 1979, I got my first leave to go home. I really enjoyed being with my family and Marlane.

On a later visit, I messed up. I was stationed at Scott Air Force Base in Bellville, Illinois. I used to go home a lot to see my girlfriend when I was there. I had caught what they called "hops." A hop is when you get on a cargo plane and do not have to pay. I would catch this flight to Wright-Patterson Air Force Base in Dayton, Ohio, and then get on another plane or the bus. I really was insecure with my relationship with Marlane because of a lack of trust.

I wanted to surprise her at her prom. I was hurt when I saw that she was with someone else. I started putting my hands on her and fighting with her. That was very bad because she ended up running as far away from me as she could get. She ended up going all the way to San Francisco with some other family members. I learned to never put my hands on a female. I ended up losing the love of my life. I was so hurt that I almost gave myself ulcers from worrying so much and stressing about what I had done.

In the air force, I was a recreation specialist. I did not have to wear a uniform. I worked at two gyms on the base, and I officiated all types of sports. I sent home all types of sports equipment to Chico. I tried to ease the pain of what I had done to Marlane by trying to talk to other women, but that did not work. I sat in my room and smoked weed to try to ease the pain. I used to cover up the smell by burning cologne in a metal pan. The military police used to bring dogs to the dorms to sniff things out, but they never caught me.

My squadron commander was from the South. She tried to get me kicked out. She had gotten at least four other black people kicked out on dishonorable discharges. She blocked my transfer to another base. I was stuck there. I decided to beat her to the punch. I explained my situation to my base commander. He let me get discharged with a general discharge under honorable conditions. I did not want her to get me out of there with a dishonorable discharge.

Chapter Six

Going Home

In January 1983, I was back in Youngstown. I felt like I had let my parents down. I decided to enroll in a technical school. I studied data processing at ITT Technical School.

Since I had to get loans for school, my mother cosigned for them. We split the money that was left over—70 percent for me and 30 percent for her. That gave me the opportunity to do what I knew best besides school. I started to sell weed, but I also smoked weed. I was my own best customer. I never made any profit because of that.

I used to smoke with my mom in her bedroom because my dad stayed down in the basement most of the time. He was there at least 90 percent of the day. I used some of the money to purchase a vehicle. When it broke down, I would walk to the Kimmel Brooks with Bumstead.

I did not graduate from ITT because of my grades in algebra and calculus. That was what I got for getting high instead of going to school and learning. I had failed myself and my parents again. So what did I do? I started experiencing with hashish, opium, acid, LSD, and THC. My dad would tell me that one drug would lead to another drug, but I was too hardheaded to listen. I had to learn the hard way. I used to go over Arthur's house. His girlfriend, Robinette Gurley, is an angel. She would always have a house full of kids helping them out with meals and a lot of love. I used to stay at their house a lot so I would not have to do so much walking. Arthur and I would sit around the house and smoke our hash and drink. Those were some very high days.

A lot of times, I would smoke with Bobwob, Arthur, and other people. It got to the point where the highs were not enough for me. I started to hang with my cousins who had cocaine all the time. I started tooting cocaine on a daily basis and would lace my joints with powder cocaine.

In 1985, people started smoking crack cocaine. I used to see how the people would be fighting over this drug and doing anything to get it. I always said that I would never start doing that drug. I had seen people die from it. Other people lost their apartments, their minds, and children.

Crack robbed people of their dignity and respect. I was raised with a lot of respect. My brothers and I would always go over to Buster and Geraldine's house on Sundays to watch football. She would always cook a meal for us. Buster, Geraldine, Larry, Arthur, my niece and nephews, and I would sit around, smoke, and eat all day long.

Chapter Seven

Losing a Sibling

I used to go out a lot after hours to Davis Night Club. My brothers used to do their other thing, but I did not indulge because I was scared. In February 1985, I went to the Davis Night Club and came home at six o'clock in the morning. My driveway was full of cars. That was not a good sign. I knew something was wrong. When I went inside, my family told me that Larry had been killed by the girlfriend that he stayed with. I was so distraught that I wanted to go kill her. I went to my car and got my sawed-off shotgun. I wanted to head down to the Kimmel Brooks to get her, but my family stopped me before I could get out the door.

People at the club were saying that I was out and did not care, but I did not know what had happened until I got home that morning. If they were so worried about me, why didn't someone come up to me and say something about it? His girlfriend did not spend a day in jail because the police had come out several times because of domestic violence incidents.

I know that she had to have had help killing him. Even though my brother was high, he was a very strong man. Arthur had to see my brother die in his arms. When she went to court, I was going wild. Her family was saying that my brother had gotten what he deserved.

After the court date, I had put together a couple of gas bombs in pop bottles. I was about to throw them at the house where I knew she was staying on the south side of town. I thought about the innocent people inside and did not do it. I put it all into God's hands.

I would toot up cocaine in my cousin's car for hours. He was one of the top dealers in the hood. All the crack heads would come see him. We used to talk about them. I would always say, "Man that is one drug that I would never do."

As time went by, I got curious about the high. I started to put the crack cocaine in my joints. We called them wooleys. There was a fine older lady whom I always liked. She was on crack. I took Buster's car to his apartment. I let her talk me into trying crack. Do not ever say never because I said that and ended up doing crack anyway.

I loved the quick high that lasted about one minute. After the initial high, we chased a ghost because that same high never came back after the first hit. We kept trying to get it. That is the insanity of that drug; you will never get that same high after the first hit. The definition of insanity is doing the same thing but expecting different results.

I had my eyes on a girl in the projects. Her name was Lashawn, but they called her Neciy. She was about eight years younger, but she had a body that wouldn't quit. I was trying to get with her, but I had a problem doing this because of our age difference. Her mom did not accept it until Neciy asked her grandmother. Her mother said that her mother told her, "If he really likes her, let them be together."

I had a problem with her stepdad. He wanted her—and she told me so. One day he chased us in my car. I got out of my car and cracked him over the head with a tire iron. He left us alone then because I went to get Buster. I knew he would have left us alone anyway because he had to take care of his bleeding head. Everyone said that the bump I put on him made it look like he had a coat rack on his head.

Neciy and I got together. We ended up having a baby boy. We named him Gary Thomas Jr. He was born on February 24, 1987. Neciy and I started having problems and did not last past his third birthday. I have moral values. I always wanted to be a family man because my mom and dad were always together and worked through their problems. That was something that Neciy did not want. I went on my way.

In 1988, I lost one of my friends to violence. Del Rio was gunned down one night as he walked on the east side. They found his body in the street in the morning. When he was killed, we were not hanging out with each other.

I had my eye on another girl from the projects. Hannah and I ended up having a child also. Quinton was born on August 3, 1989. He did not have my last name because Hannah and I were having some problems. I was not there when he was born.

I found out that she was cheating on me after I got her pregnant. I should have known it because every time I wanted to come over, I had to call first. I ended up having two sons with different mothers. I was with Gary's mom for three years, and I was with Quinton's mom for two years.

I had always wanted to raise a family like my parents had, but I stopped having kids after that second try. I did not want my kids scattered around. I ended up chasing away both of my sons' mothers because I thought it was okay to fight them and get physical. That was what I had seen growing up.

After Quinton was born, I went over Hannah's house without calling. I found out that she had someone else in the house. I got so upset that I slapped her with a book. She started chasing me with a butcher knife. I ran out of the house, but she continued chasing me. Since I was high at the time, my wind was really short.

She caught up with me around one of the apartment buildings. She started stabbing me. She caught me on my head. I fell to the ground and covered my head, but she kept swinging the knife. I was begging for my life. I started having flashbacks about how my brother Larry had died. I started telling her that. I called out to Jesus Christ to please help me.

She kept swinging until her brother, Alto, came to my rescue. If it was not for him, I believe she would have killed me. I believe Jesus Christ heard me and sent him to rescue me. I would have bled to death if people hadn't told me to go look at my head. I used my T-shirt to cover up my wound. After forty-five minutes, I decided to look at it in the mirror. I realized that I had better go to the hospital. The doctor told me that if I had not come, I would have bled to death. If the knife had caught me just an eighth of an inch over, I would have died. The wound required nine stitches on the inside and twelve on the outside.

Thank God for Jesus! The violence was always around me.

Chapter Eight

An Escalated Drug Life

We used to find empty apartments to get high. I also lived in one for a while. I used to go trick with the crack heads. Bobwob and I would do our thing with smoking, but I did not get high with hard legs. That was not my thing. My thing was getting high with soft legs. When I got high, I always wanted to have oral sex—and no man could do that for me. When I got high, I got horny. I wanted to be around females so I could get what I wanted. He would have his, and I would have mine. When I was thirty years old, my life took a serious turn. I got into life-or-death situations, and my nickname played a big part in my life. I had keys to some empty apartments, and I could go in them when I got ready. I tricked with a lot of females, but there were only a few that I went inside of. I did not trust too many of them. I didn't know who they had been with. All they could do for me was give me oral sex. There were several that I did go in because I wanted them to see how I was. The ones from high school that played hard to get, but some of them were too good for me then, but look at you now. This went on for a while. I always had the drug because I had an enabler in my life.

My cousin always made sure that I had drugs because he was a big dealer. All I had to do was bring him back his money for his ounces to get more. I made sure to always have his money, but I would trick off the rest. I would always walk around the projects, shaking my pill bottles full of rocks.

I was also one of the top crack dealers in the hood because of the way I did business. I treated my customers like I wanted to be treated—with a lot of love. I even had crack from other dealers that I competed with because of my name.

In 1990, I learned how to cook powder cocaine to crack. I was one of the best cookers in the projects. All of the dealers would come to me to cook for them. I was getting all types of dope to do my thing. My nickname was "Crack."

The dealers would give me some of their dope to sell because they knew how much I could make on the streets. I could make $1,000 in six hours. I had to take some time off during the day to trick some of it off.

The task force used to make their rounds in the hood, but I never got caught with it. We always had people looking out for the police. We had many escape routes that we could take. One day, we were getting high in an empty apartment after a task force raid. Bumstead came into the apartment to get high. Then there was a knock on the door by one of the hood drug dealers. They had confronted Bumstead about picking up their dope, but he said that he had not picked it up.

I believed him because he would have told me the truth. The drug dealer asked him to come outside to show him where he had run from. I heard a gunshot and knew he had shot Bumstead. I went outside and saw him on the ground with a gunshot wound. He had trouble breathing. I knew right then that he was not going to make it. He died on the way to the hospital.

Chapter Nine

Drugs and Violence

I became really popular in a short period of time. People used to ask for me by name. They would not buy from anyone unless they had seen me. I had so much dope because the other dealers would give me theirs too.

Some of them would say, "How can he always have crack and be on crack?"

Since my cousin always kept me supplied, I had more dope to smoke up. My habit had gotten so bad that I made no profit from selling—maybe a few dollars to buy some beer or something. I was making at least $2,000 a day for the dealers. I had even stopped paying rent to my dad, and he had kicked me out of the house. My mom tried to save me from being kicked out, but I left because I did not want them fighting over their crack head son.

I was in my own hometown with all my family, but I was homeless—a homeless drug dealer! I did end up staying with Bobwob for a while. I also ended up getting some more apartment keys from some of my crack head associates. My habit got really, really bad. I started to mess up some of the dealer's money to keep supplying my habit. My cousin got mad and stopped giving me all those ounces because he did not see me gaining anything from it.

I eventually messed up the wrong person's money. I came up about $160 short for him, but I had sold about $16,000. I thought I could be all right with that. He and three friends came looking for me. They ended up finding me at one of my crack head associate's apartment. They took me out of the apartment by gunpoint and into their car. I was in the middle of the backseat with a gun pointed at my side. We drove away from the projects. They were saying, "How does it feel to know that you are getting ready to die, MF?" I was shaking like a crap game.

I tried to tell them that I could get the money from someone, but they did not want to hear that. They drove me to a wooded area on the Sharon Line. They kept teasing me about dying. They took me out of the car and started beating on me. I fought back for a hot second, but I could not fight four people. I dropped to the ground and curled up. They stopped fighting and the guy I owed money to went back to the car and got his .38. He stood back and shot me through my right ankle. I staggered into the woods to get away. He shot a second time and the bullet went through my left calf. I staggered deeper into the woods and he pointed the gun at my chest.

I hollered, "Jesus Christ, please help me."

One of his friends grabbed him and said, "Man, let's go. Somebody probably heard us."

After they left, I crawled out to the street.

I know that there is power in Jesus' name. When I called out his name, he sent down an angel to save me. Since I did not see any houses, I crawled up the street about 100 yards until I saw a house with a light on. I crawled to the house, banged on the door, and cried for help. They would not let me in, but I know that they called for help because I heard sirens coming down the street.

I crawled back into the street so the police and the ambulance would see me. They were talking to me the whole time so that I would not go to sleep.

To this day, I am grateful for our Lord and Savior, Jesus Christ, because he actually saved my life. I am also grateful for the people in the house that called 911. The dealer contacted me while I was in the hospital. He was trying to get me not to blame him. He had been arrested about two weeks after the shooting. He sent people to the hospital to say that he would pay me not to testify against him. He offered me an ounce, but I said no.

I stayed in the hospital for a month. I had to have a cast put on my right leg. I had to get artificial veins put in my left leg. My legs still give out on me at times—and I sometimes fall.

The Lord put my sister in my life again. Shirley and her friend let me stay with them when I was released from the hospital. I had to learn to walk again. I had to crawl all over my sister's house to get around.

At Shirley's house, I decided to take his bribe. I was getting fended out to smoke again. I got in touch with him to let him know that I would take the ounce of powder cocaine. I ended up sneaking out of my sister's house to meet him. I was on crutches in the projects—and doing my thing all over again.

When it came time for me to testify, I said they had the wrong man. The court knew that I had been paid off because they asked how much I had received to say this. The state ended up taking the case, and they sentenced him anyway. After a while I healed and could walk without the crutches.

Chapter Ten

The Violence Continues

During the summer of 1991, one of the most notorious criminals in our town got out of prison. He was known for killing people and getting away with it. He had seen me and wanted to talk to me. We had grown up together, but he did crime and I did not. He was Bobwob's cousin.

When we finally talked, he told me how my name was ringing in the prison. They knew I was a top crack seller. He wanted to get with me so I could help him do his thing. With my desperate urge to get high, I started to sell for him so that I could supply my habit. I ended up messing his money up too!

I know the good Lord was watching over me. I sold for him for two months before I went in debt to him. I used to get money from some of my female customers to offset what I owed him. I did this until I relied on a couple of them—and they did not come through for me. I would get their money and put them on hold until I got my dope from him—and then I would give them their dope.

When it caught up to me, I ended up owing him about $250. My sick mind was telling me that after making him about $100,000, I could be short that amount and be okay.

I was out hustling in the projects to get his money together. He sent a hit after me to get his money or kill me. He sent a teenage girlfriend of his to do this while he went after other people who owed him.

She jumped out of her car and said, "Crack, where is his money at?" She pointed a semiautomatic pistol at me from close range and pulled the trigger. The gun jammed and did not fire. She kept trying to shoot me, but it would not shoot. I took off running through the projects. I had just gotten off my crutches. People told me that I was running so fast they could not believe it.

When you are scared, you can be amazed by what you can do. I knew that Jesus Christ was with me once again. When I was running, everybody that I trusted was slamming doors in my face. I kept running through the projects until I saw an open door.

I ran in the apartment. I know this was an act of God because the elderly woman who barely knew me let me in. Her daughter and I explained what was happening. I stayed with her for almost a month afraid that he would find me.

I asked Arthur to tell the dealer I would get the money. He suggested that I continue to sell for him without getting any profit. I was taking too long for him; he told me he had something for me to do. He wanted me to rob a dope house and kill the people inside.

I was scared. If I didn't do it, he'd kill me. I had gone to school with the people he was talking about. I had never killed anyone before. I was messing with a girl whose sister was selling out of her house.

The night I was supposed to do it, I went into hiding again. I surfaced after a couple of days. I found out that they went into another dope house and robbed and killed four people. That was Labor Day of 1991.

That next morning, I saw him as he rode through the projects. He stopped his car and told me he'd be back in a minute. He was with the girl he had sent to kill me. I was scared to death, but he never made it back because friends of the people he had killed went after him in their cars. They chased him and had a little shootout, but he had got away.

A young boy had told everyone in the projects that I was involved in that massacre. Another guy I had grown up with was trying to say the same thing. I believe that they were trying to implicate me because I was taking away some of their crack sales. Hating on me was their way to get rid of me.

I had all these people looking to kill me for no reason. I was hiding from the guy. How could I be with him?

I am so thankful for our Lord and Savior, Jesus Christ. He put someone else in my life to protect me. Robinette's brother let me stay with him until I could find somewhere else to go. I had to get away as far as I could. I was on the run again.

I got in touch with my uncle, Buster, and Arthur. They stayed on the north side of town and I was on the east side. My uncle took some money to my brothers so I could leave town. At night, I had to sneak my way across town to Buster's house. He and Arthur took me to the bus station.

Chapter Eleven

Fleeing from Violence

I called a dear friend of mine from high school. He resided in San Francisco. He said it was all right for me to visit him, but I did not tell him what was going on. I had been on the bus for three days and had twenty dollars in my pocket. I tried to spend it wisely, but the places the bus stopped were very expensive.

When I arrived in San Francisco, I had three dollars. I called my friend to let him know I was there. The first thing he said was that I could not stay with him because the people who were after me could have followed me.

How he found out was beyond me, but word of mouth really travels fast. I was 3,500 miles away from home. I stayed in the bus station for a couple of days. I started walking around to see where I could get help. I had found out where I could get a meal and shelter. I stood in soup lines and stayed at the Salvation Army. I was in the Tenderloin District. I was not used to seeing districts. I was used to east side, north side, south side, and west side.

I ended up finding a job with my mom's help. She pretended to be a café called Mom's. I asked her to be my job reference. Boudin's Bakery and Café was opening up. I told my mom that they might call her. She did the right thing, and they hired me as a dishwasher. I ended up meeting a white girl named Kiplee Johnson. She helped me in a lot of ways, but I still wanted to get high and was hiding it from her.

I even met her dad; he was a medical correspondent for ABC television. She had money, but she was very humble. Nobody would believe that she had money like that because she did not show it. She used to take me around the city. San Francisco is beautiful—and expensive. I learned my way around and found where the crack was. I ended up finding a one-room apartment in the Tenderloin. I ended up homeless again because I got behind in my rent. Since I did not want Kiplee to know, I started sleeping in the bus station and under bridges.

I kept my job so that I could supply my habit. I was in and out of shelters and rooms for about seven months. I got so desperate that I ate out of garbage cans. Do not ever say what you will not do to survive. San Francisco has its own rules and laws. If you stepped on a piece of sidewalk that a homeless person was using, they would cuss you out and tell you to get out of their house.

I once saw a naked lady in a lawn chair; she was washing up with a washcloth. People were acting like this was normal.

Other people were smoking crack by the police substation. The police would ride by and do nothing. The jails were overcrowded—maybe that was why they were so bold.

I used to ride Bay Area Rapid Transit to Oakland. I got my weed there. I found out about this from a friend from back home. I understood why he would not let me stay with him. I had stayed with his aunt, but I had messed that up because of drugs. Drugs will tear your life apart if you let them. I give all my thanks to God for being there for me. I thank him for his grace and mercy!

I would just ride the bus to waste time. The cost of living was too expensive for me. My room was costing me about $500—and I had to share my bathroom with the entire floor. I ended up seeing Marlane there several times, but she was in a relationship with someone else.

I started to get homesick.

Chapter Twelve

Going Home Again

In April 1992, I called Arthur to see if they were still looking for me. I was sending money home to my uncle to save for me because I knew if I kept it, the money would go toward more crack. He told me that word had gotten around that I had not been involved in the killings. It was all right for me to come home.

On my first day back, I went over a friend's house to get high. These friends were some of the ones I used to get high with in the projects. And as soon as I took my first hit, I heard a loud gunshot. It sounded close.

A guy said, "Where that mf at?"

Within seconds, a big guy with a gun was trying to get inside the house. I told him not to panic and unlock the back door. He had about four locks on the door. I thought I was dead, but he got it open. I ended up running for my life again.

I went to Bobwob's house to tell him what was going on. He told everyone that I had nothing to do with those killings. Word got out around the hood, and I eventually went back outside.

I stayed with Bobwob for a while and then ended up moving in with Neciy. I thought I would give it another chance with her. I stopped getting high for once.

I prayed and cried out to God to release me from this habit. I knew that I could not do it on my own. I prayed to God to take away my urge to smoke crack—and I was done with it the next morning. Thanks to God and my Lord and Savior, Jesus Christ, and the Holy Spirit.

Chapter Thirteen

Starting a Crack-Free Life

I went job hunting to help support my two sons. I ended up getting a job at North Star Steel from a temporary agency. I worked outside loading steel tubing on trailers. I ended up moving Neciy and her kids into a house, but our relationship didn't work out because her sister was getting into our business. I went to stay with Buster and his girlfriend on the north side. I ended up getting a nice Cadillac.

I was going out to the projects to show off my car and how far I had come in life with the Lord's blessings. I started to attend church every Sunday to show my thanks for all that the Lord had done for me and the blessings I received. The church was called The Lighthouse. My brother-in-law, Bruce Abbott, was the pastor. I knew that God could transform lives because Bruce was a former drug user. When he appointed me trustee over the financial affairs, I felt like I was somebody.

I stopped going to church because the pastor was not there anymore. I had an excuse. The one thing that I have learned is that the enemy never ceases to attack someone who is trying to live a Christian lifestyle because we look too much like Christ.

One day, a young guy came up to me and said, "How did you come from out of town and get a good job and a nice car? You must be a snitch."

I told him these things could happen for him if he knew Jesus Christ like I did—and then I called him uneducated. He got mad and told someone else that I was a snitch or something. Me, Bobwob, his brother, and another friend went up the street to get in my car.

We saw someone walking toward the car with an assault rifle. I asked him not to shoot. He shot into the driver's side—where I was—about five times, but no bullets hit anyone. I sped off.

The Lord was protecting us. When I returned the next day in my bullet-riddled Cadillac, the young guys started ducking and hiding. They thought I was coming to retaliate. I just wanted to talk to them. We settled the situation, but my car was messed up.

North Star Steel hired me in August 1992. I was not getting high—at least not on crack. I was drinking and smoking weed. I ended up trading my Cadillac for a new car. That really pissed people off.

In January 1993, Kiplee asked me to come to Boston to meet her parents. I went up there for about a month to get away. I used some vacation time and sick days. I also visited New Hampshire where they had a vacation home. They were living large.

Chapter Fourteen

Back to Crack

After a year, I began to use crack again. I was making good money at my new job. I had a dangerous job in the melt shop. We had to wear 100 percent cotton thermals year round because of the heat. We used to see tissue paper ignite just from being on the floor. We would melt down scrap steel with an oxygen lance to turn it to molten steel. We would tap out the furnace with temperatures up to 3,500 degrees. I used to go straight to work from the streets. We worked a swing shift.

In December 1993, my nephew Booney came from Southern California to stay with his dad, Buster. We used to get high almost every day. In January, we picked up one of his friends to ride with us. We decided to get some drinks and play cards at Booney's cousin's house. His friend dropped five valiums into a pint of Thunderbird and drank it all—except for a little bit that he gave Booney. His friend started playing with his 9mm Glock gun at the card table. He said, "You know what? I want to do what they did in *Menace to Society*." I paid him no attention.

When we ran out of drinks, I offered to go back to the store for more. I went to the store with my nephew and his friend. We all went inside, and we all left at the same time. My nephew's friend said he had forgotten to do something. He went back into the store, and I heard gunshots, so I pulled off. I tried to go back to the store, but the street was blocked off by the police. He had gone back inside and killed the two owners. I was so scared that I went home.

That night, the police arrested my nephew. His friend was on the run. In the morning, the detectives picked me up at work and confiscated my car. They told me that I would be charged with complicity to murder—and I could get the same amount of time as the shooter. I was praying all the way downtown. A small still voice told me to tell the truth and nothing but the truth. When we got downtown, I told them the truth. They had me sign a paper saying that I would not be charged with the crime. Telling the truth shall set you free.

God knows that we had nothing to do with it, but my nephew served two months before they let him go. They caught his friend in another city; he is doing life for the crime he committed. He got word back to me that he was putting a hit on me to not testify. He even had a picture of me circulating in the hood. I do not know how he got the picture, but I have an idea. To stop the pressure on Buster and Rita, I ended up moving out. I went to stay with Robinette; she was a godsend. She would always help me in my time of need.

When the court date arrived, he was trying to give me a hard look, but I gave it back to him. I said, "You do not scare me. You did the crime, so you do the time. Why should an innocent person suffer because of you?"

In 2010, he was put to death for that crime. I could have been charged with the same crime, but a voice told me that the truth would set me free. I did not have to do the time for this crime because I was innocent. I was only giving him a ride to the store—but that could have been my life too. Always keep God in your life. You never know what will happen in the future, but God has the last say in all matters.

I started getting high on crack again—and it escalated to a much higher level. I needed more to get high with. In February, I took some vacation time because my mom had gotten sick. I wanted to spend some time with her. She was on dialysis for a while. When she knew I was attending church, she was all right. When I had stopped and started getting high again, she got sicker.

I was her baby—the youngest of us all. Mothers know when a child is doing well or not. You cannot fool your mom. I spent every one of my vacation days with her at the hospital. They had to do an operation on her cancer. I watched her age years in a matter of a couple weeks. She passed away in February.

The whole family came up to the hospital, and we watched her take her last breath. Sometimes I feel that I was the cause of her dying. If I had only left that crack alone, I believe she would have lived a little longer. I think I contributed to her broken heart. If I had known, I would have cried out to my Lord and Savior, Jesus Christ, again!

In April 1994, I lost my job at North Star Steel. They gave me a drug test in March, and I came back positive for cocaine. I feel they were picking on me because it was on the news when I was arrested. It was not good for them to have a murder suspect working at their site. That is the reason they sent me for testing.

It got to the point where I was sick and tired of being sick and tired. I got my retirement check from North Star Steel for $780, and I had to buy my youngest son a bike for his birthday in August. I had decided to go get a hit of crack before I went bike shopping.

I took that first hit, and I never did get the bike. I smoked up my entire check.

Chapter Fifteen

My Last Days of Crack

I was sick and tired of letting the devil get the best of me. I decided to admit myself to a rehab facility for help. My flesh was just too weak at that time because I had not given my life over to God.

I needed help because I was tired of neglecting my two sons for my habit. I decided to spend three months in the Donofrio Home in October. I learned about the twelve step program and how it worked. We went to meetings every day. I was in the process of getting my life back in order. I met a few people I used to get high with, but the program tells you to change the people you hang around with and your surroundings. I used to give what they called a lead at meetings. I stood in front of a lot of addicts and told my story. People in the audience used to cry as I told my story. Many of them would tell me that I needed to write a book about my life so I could save someone that was on drugs.

We went to church on Sundays in rehab. On one Sunday, Pastor Selena Covington came down from her pulpit and said, "Son, there is a calling for you to save people. The Lord wants to use you because you have an attractiveness about you—if you don't let the devil rob you of it."

Out of all the people in church that Sunday, she interrupted her service to tell me that. I had been letting Satan rob me for years. Eighteen years have passed since she told me that. Now I am getting my book out. It is not to glorify me; it is to glorify our Lord and Savior, Jesus Christ. It is not about me—it is about him! Linda was one of the good people I met in rehab. After we got out, she used to pick me up for the meetings.

When I got out of rehab three months later, I did what I was not supposed to do. I had hooked up with a girl in there. When we had both gotten out, I decided to live with Yvonne. What a mistake! The program tells you not to have a relationship while you are in there. When we got out, it was not long before I started to get high again.

My habit quickly escalated to a high level. I needed more—and I also started hearing voices and feeling paranoid. I was sick and tired of letting the drug control my life. I didn't enjoy the high because I was window shopping every time I took a hit. Yvonne was back on it too, and she was staying away from the house for days at a time. I thought she would change her ways because she had to raise her two boys. She went back to the drugs and would leave them with me for days. I had gotten tired of the drugs.

Since I had to get away, the Lord put my sister back in my life. My family had been done with me because of my constant drug use. Shirley took me in when I told her that I wanted to change my life. She saw the hurt in my eyes. I decided to do my own rehab with the help of God, since I knew what I had learned at the rehab center.

I stopped getting high on March 12, 1995. I haven't used crack since, but I give all the thanks to the Donofrio Home, my Father in heaven, his son, Jesus Christ, and the Holy Spirit. People can work the twelve step program, but I feel that you only have to take one step. Take that step and believe in God. I thank God for Jesus Christ for shedding his blood on Calvary for all of our sins. Having faith in him is what keeps me going today!

I asked people to call me Gary; I was no longer "Crack." After living with my sister for three months, I decided to get my own place. In May of 1996, I was approved to live in a project called the Victory Annex on the east side of town. I was not using drugs, but I decided to sell them again. My business was booming, and everyone was coming to me. I took over the Victories for a hot minute—until the young boys decided that I was taking money from them.

I had my sons and nephews over to my place for the night. I took Jermaine home; we called him "Nukes." When I got back to my apartment and shut the door, my apartment was riddled with fifteen rounds of bullets. Nobody was hit. I thanked God for saving me. If the shooters had been serious, they could have gunned me down before I even got to my door. When I went to get some guns and family, they broke into my apartment. They ransacked, and I did not want to deal with fixing it. I took my important stuff and went to think things out at a hotel.

When I moved to the Victories, I started talking to Rachell Lynn McCoy. After two weeks in the hotel, we decided to move to Columbus. My niece Shawnya used to go there a lot. She told me how many jobs were there.

Our Lord and Savior, Jesus Christ, saved me from so many situations that I knew I had to leave the drug life alone or die doing it. There were only two outcomes for that lifestyle: hell or jail. I didn't choose either one.

Chapter Sixteen

My New Lifestyle

I was ready for a drug-free life. I wanted to make my money legally. I did not want to look over my shoulder for the police or someone who was out to get me. We drove to Columbus in October of 1996—and I have not looked back since then.

We stayed in a hotel when we first arrived. We looked for work the next day, and we both found a job at the same place. It was through a temporary agency that did not last long, but jobs were so plentiful that we could leave one job and go to another one.

I found the perfect job. It was getting paid by piece rate, which is getting paid by the amount of work you put out per hour. I was making $15 per hour doing this; I have my dad's blood. He used to work like crazy. When we needed money for our hotel room, we would borrow from my mom's brother.

When we got tired of sleeping in the hotel, we went looking for a place to stay. We ended up finding a place called Greenbrier Apartments on the east side of town. I always end up staying on the east side of town. We did not know the area at all. We moved to a place called "Oozy Alley" because of all the violence that happened there—no wonder it was so easy for us to get in there.

We went back to Youngstown for the Christmas holiday. I saw on the news that they kicked in someone's door and killed her. On my way to work one day, a young guy approached me to sell some drugs. I told him that I did not want any drugs because I did not get high anymore. He told me that I would buy some drugs from him whether I liked it or not. I asked the landlord if we could get out of our lease, but they would let us out of it. We tried to find another apartment to no avail.

In March, we were still looking for a place. We ended up getting someone to cosign for us so that we could move away from that mess. The place was so bad that most cabs would not even go there. We had to beg them to take us in there, and they would practically throw us out the cab. I did not want to stay there. I had just left that life and would be damned if we had come all that way just to live the same way.

Shawnya cosigned for us after I told her about our living conditions. We moved into a complex called Beacon Hill in a much safer neighborhood. Lynn and I went to Youngstown to get her children, Christopher and Lucy. My son, Lil Gary was shuttled back and forth for several years. I tried showing him love, but Gary would always want to run back to Youngstown. Sometimes you have to show your child tough love so they will not try to run you over.

I tried to help other family members get away from Youngstown. The only one that stayed was Shawnya. Lynn and I were having hard times because I had not known her that well before we moved to Columbus. I did not go out to the clubs, and she did. We used to argue a lot about that, but I tried my best to make the relationship work because I loved her.

We had a lot of differences because of our lifestyles. When you love someone as much as I loved Lynn, you try to work out your problems. My dad got sick after he had a stroke. Chico was staying with him at the time. He and Neecee were helping him out a lot. When he suffered a second stroke, he lost all of his mobility.

After his first stroke, Neecee would feed him and take him where he needed to go. After his second one, he lost everything—even his sight was going. Neecee did all that she could for him, but she had to put him in a nursing facility. We would drive to Youngstown to visit him on weekends. I hated seeing him in that condition. I loved him very much, and I wanted him to know it.

After a couple of months, Neecee couldn't go see him every day. He was being neglected. Nursing facilities are not the best thing, but sometimes you have to put your loved ones in these places. Since he was not getting the proper care in Youngstown,

I decided to ask the family to move him to Columbus for better care. It took a lot to convince my dad to move, but he agreed.

Brian and I drove my dad to Columbus. I was worried for him. I wanted him to get better care, but I found out that all nursing homes are the same. I took him from one nursing home to another. I used to visit him every day with Shirley. Shawnya would visit him a lot also. It was very hard to watch him suffer. I prayed to the Lord to take my father out of his misery. After six months in Columbus, he passed away. It was the week of Thanksgiving of 1999. I watched him take his last breaths.

I'll never forget him looking at me and shedding tears. At least I was able to kiss him and tell him that I loved him. When I was telling him that I loved him, he would shed another tear. As I am writing this, I am in tears because I feel that the devil took him away from me during my addiction to drugs. I care now! God bless his soul! I love you, Mom and Dad!

My addiction to drugs really altered my mind and my thinking. Drugs made me do some perverted things. When you are on drugs, you are not in your right state of mind. Drugs make you do things that you would not if you were clean and sober. There are so many people I have hurt through my addiction. I am very sorry to everyone I have hurt because of my actions. I pray that whoever I have hurt in the past will have the heart to forgive me for my actions. Who are we not to forgive since God has forgiven us all for our sins? We must all have the heart to forgive because we all have faults.

I was trying to get my life back on track after my parents took their last breaths. It was very hard to get through, but I give all the praises and glory to Jesus Christ who brought me through all of this.

In 2000, Lynn and I had our first child. On July 5, Raquan M. Thomas was born. We were doing all right, but we were having some problems. I started getting high again—but not with cocaine. I figured I would be all right just smoking weed. I was upset with Lynn for going out to the clubs, but I was at fault just as much because I sometimes dropped her off at the clubs. I did not want to be arguing—and I had trust in her.

The one thing that makes a relationship work is trust; without trust, you have no relationship. We ended up leaving Beacon Hill in 2001 because we needed more room. Gary was living with us. Her children, Lucy and Chris, were also with us. We moved to the Hamilton Arms Apartments. In 2002, Raeniqua E. Thomas was born on March 15. We call her "Little Mama" because she shared my mothers' birthday. Our relationship was not working, but I was holding on to her for some reason.

Things were not working out financially, and we ended up losing our apartment. A friend of Lynn's found us a house a few blocks away on Carlton Road. We were doing a little better in our relationship, but Chris started acting up. The juvenile system became involved in our mess, and we had to release him to them to help him with discipline. He ended up learning about reality and getting his life together. We moved again; Rustic Ridge was a few blocks away.

In 2004, Rashun L. Thomas was born. All of our kids are very respectful and have moral values. He ended up getting into trouble for not doing well in school. We tried to scare him straight. I knew a guy that worked in the juvenile system. He was from Youngstown. I asked him to talk to Gary about the consequences of not doing well in school and what would happen if he did not do the right thing in school. He did his best to scare him straight, but it only worked for a little while. I tried my best to teach Gary the right things, but he kept running back to Youngstown.

You have to show your kids tough love so that they know what is right and what is wrong. Gary ended up breaking into an apartment. He tried to deny it, but there were too many witnesses—even my son and others saw him do it. When I tried talking to him, he got irate and started saying bad things to me. I knew he did not mean what he said.

When he ran back to Youngstown, there ended up being a warrant for his arrest. I tried talking to him about turning himself in. He ended up getting into trouble again, and the law brought him back to Columbus. We had to move again—Gary ended up staying with us in Coventry East Apartments. He got into more trouble with the law and ran back to Youngstown again.

There was another warrant for his arrest. The law came to our apartment early in the morning to try to catch him. He did something else in Youngstown and was sent back to Columbus. He had so many chances to turn his life around for the better, but a hard head makes a soft ass. I said, "Do your time—and get yourself together. Pray to God for deliverance of your soul because the only reading material I will bring you while you are incarcerated is the Holy Bible."

Lynn and I are doing much better in our relationship, and I owe it all to God. I continued to hold onto his mercy and grace, and he kept me. He has taken away my desire to smoke weed and drink. Lynn and I decided to get married in 2009. We worked through a lot of issues in the past thirteen years. It is time to get married so that we are right in the eyes of God!

A friend from Columbus knew someone with a childcare business. They needed someone to take care of their books. Since I had gone to ITT and had been doing taxes since 1986, our finances started getting better. Our family was doing well and we moved to Tuxworth Drive. The lady that I was working for knew the landlord and gave her my name.

While I was working at the daycare, a female employee started harassing me. She wanted me to start a sexual relationship with her. I took this situation to the owners of the business, but they did nothing to prevent this employee from messing with me. I had to take it a step further and reported it to the Ohio Civil Rights Commission. As soon as the owners found out what I'd done, they cut my hours from eighty hours every two weeks to twelve hours every two weeks. When I came to work the next day, they terminated my employment. The landlord told us we had to move again.

I gave my life to Jesus on April 12, 2009. I have been clean since that day. No matter which one it is, drugs alter your mind.

Chapter Seventeen

My Life with Our Savior, Jesus Christ

My new life depends on Jesus Christ. He guides me with the Holy Spirit that dwells inside me so that I may live for him and inherit the Kingdom of God for my eternity.

When I prayed to the Lord on April 12, 2009, he took the desire away from me! Now I am totally drug free! I have found a very great church named Praise and Worship Deliverance Center. Lynn was still going out to the clubs, but I continued to go to church and prayed for her deliverance. I was taking our kids to see if it would rub off on her to come, but it did not happen.

When we had to move from Tuxworth Drive, I rented a U-Haul truck. The oldest elder of my church, Elder Barbara Keaton, saw us at my nephew Derrick's (Chico) thrift store. She wanted to talk to Lynn because I was always telling her how I wanted Lynn to come to church. I had the pastor—and everyone else in the church—praying for me. No one can tell me about the power of prayer because all the praying finally touched my fiancée. Since Elder Keaton invited her to Praise and Worship Deliverance Center, she has not stopped attending.

We are going to church as a family should. This is the first church that I can go to and be taught the Word. The pastor, Ronnie K. Reed, keeps it real. He does not beat around the bush. He takes time out of his busy schedule to help his members. Since he is a Bishop-Elect, he has been consecrated as Bishop Ronnie K. Reed on November 16, 2009! At Praise and Worship Deliverance Cathedral, we have a humble bishop as our shepherd. There are not many pastors who will take the time to have a friendly relationship with his congregation. He helps us go with him. When he preaches, he has me in tears because of his caring spirit.

God blesses you, Bishop Ronnie K. Reed and First Lady Tina. I have feelings and a loving heart for people again in my life. I'm able to do things now that I could not do before. I can appreciate my life and my ability to support my family. I can go to the store whenever I feel like it. I can make promises to people and keep them. I don't have to look over my shoulder to see if someone is after me or feel paranoid. I can care for people and help them when they need it. I know how to enjoy life and have fun with a sober mind. I can remember what I did the day before.

I have settled down in Columbus. I work legally for a living. I have a peace of mind. With all I have been through, I know that an angel watches over me. I could have been killed more than three times, but my Lord and Savior, Jesus Christ, has plans for me. I pray that all people on crack cocaine will believe and have faith to see the wondrous works that can be done to them. I thought I would never leave drugs alone. Now I have my life back—and even my name back. I can be called Gary again. Once you have been saved and surrender all to Jesus Christ, you become new. People say, "Once a crack head, always a crack head." They must not know the God I serve.

The Lord has given me strength to keep me strong. If I had to rely upon my own strength, I would be too weak to stay sober. I tell everyone to have and keep the faith in our Lord Jesus Christ. For whomsoever shall trust in the lord will be with the lord. Anyone who is doing crack and wants to get out of that life of misery should repent and turn to our Lord. Rehabilitation centers will change their lives, but we only have to give one step and that is to God Almighty. The twelve step programs will help you stay clean and sober—if you work at it. They teach you what to do and what not to do when you go back into the real world. Don't start a relationship during rehab—especially with someone that's going through the same thing you are. I went right back into the ugly world of crack cocaine, but I was taught enough.

With the strength of my higher power, I pulled away from the madness and did what was required to stay clean and sober. I give the entire honor to my Lord and Savior, Jesus Christ!

On December 5, 2009, Lynn and I got married! I thank God for turning our lives around. I give thanks to my church family for being there for us as we continue to grow in Jesus Christ. We are not perfect, but God is still working on us. He is still building the church inside of us so we can share our life so others can see how great God is. If I have hurt anyone in any way, I do apologize and ask for forgiveness. God has forgiven us for our sins so we can live a productive and prosperous life. I thank God for Bishop Ronnie K. Reed, Elder Tina Reed, and the Praise and Worship family.

We have to pray for a discerning spirit so we can know what is from the heart and what is merely words coming out of somebody's mouth. My family really liked our church, but there were times when we had to leave because not everyone had the same agenda. God said, "Love one another as I love you."

We faced many attacks from the congregation because of the way we presented ourselves. We were not liked because we always dressed nicely as a family. It is sad to say, but they looked at us like we thought we were better than others. They did not understand that it was how we dressed when we were out in the world. Why would we change to come into the kingdom of God? We felt so good inside that it showed on the outside. As a family, we all love God, but we have to be careful of the haters inside of the church because some people have different agendas. We have to be careful of the shepherd of the sheep to know that he is doing God's business, which is winning lost souls into the kingdom of God.

I study Christian Ministry and Leadership at Ohio Christian University. I am finding out that there are some things that we need to fine tune as a whole body of Christ. We cannot be hypocrites in church. We should not say we love God and not display our love to others in the church. It is not just about attending the church—God tells us to have love for each other. This is what shows our accountability to him.

God does not want us to be lukewarm for him. He wants us on fire for him so that we can profess his goodness throughout all nations. I am praying that our church as a whole will start to display unity inside and outside the church because it is about God's business. When we wake up as a whole body of Christ, God will step in and bless the church with the mission he has in store for us.

I am constantly in prayer because I have a loving heart. When I say that I love you, I mean it from the inside of my soul. I am not just saying the words to be heard. It is all about doing God's business. I am saying, "Wake up! Tomorrow is not promised to anybody. We have to live each day like it is our last." If you died today, where would you go?

Bishop Reed is trying his best to teach unity inside the church. We need to hear his cry. He knows this is where we should be in order for us to all go together in unity. God is coming back for a church with no blemish or wrinkle. We all hear the good Word of God that he preaches to us, but we need to be doers of the Word.

We, as a family, are at the point where we need to take a stand. Do not let the members who are not in Christ interrupt our salvation. Some will try to steal your joy because they are not rooted and grounded in the Word. The church is a spiritual hospital that will heal the ones who seek God diligently and with patience for him to do work within us.

I am still going through a transformation inside my body, mind, and soul, but I will continue to press my way in for the promises of God. We have to pray because they are human just like us. Never put mankind above our Father in heaven. He is a jealous god.

This is my everyday prayer:

> Lord, I ask you in the name of Jesus, that you come into the hearts and minds of our congregation to let them know of your glory and grace and that we are not in some type of game to be played for this is so real, and I do not want any of us to miss the prize that awaits us in heaven. In Jesus' name, I pray. Amen!

I would like to add a few poems that my wonderful wife wrote. They really touched my heart because we both possess a kind, loving spirit for everybody that we come into contact with. We are very humble people, and God knows that we speak is from the depths of our hearts and minds.

It's Time

It's time for me to turn and say that the devil no longer stands in my way.
It's time for me to surrender to all and give up my heart for the Lord to rule.
He's stopping the evil from blocking my vision.
I'll serve the Lord;
I'll make it my mission.
He's opening my eyes and letting me see his amazing grace and his love for me.
The power of his love runs deep in my veins.
I'll shout to the world, "It's the Lord who reigns."
God willingly surrendered his son for me;
I will proceed to love him eternally.
The work of the devil is all around;
He kills, destroys, but I'm standing my ground.
I won't give up.
I said, "I won't give up; I won't let him win,"
For the gates of true love have let me back in.

I Thank You, Lord

I thank you, Lord, for your love and your glory.
I thank you, Lord, so I can tell my story.
I thank you, Lord, for taking away the hurt and the pain and allowing me to praise your Holy name.
I thank you, Lord, for allowing me to smile and laugh and leading me down that righteous path.
I thank you, Lord, for allowing me to believe so I can do all the things I need to achieve.
I thank you, Lord, for letting me see that all you want is the best for me.
I thank you, Lord, for trials and tribulations so one day I can preach to all nations.
I thank you, Lord, for taking me off the streets and putting the devil under my feet.
I thank you, Lord, for allowing me to pray and believing your word and your amazing grace.
I thank you, Lord, for the sun, moon, and stars above.
Most of all, I thank you, Lord, for your love.

I Refuse to Be Discouraged

I refuse to be discouraged, to be sad, or to cry.
I refuse to be downhearted, and here's the reason why:
I have a God who's mighty;
He's loveable and supreme.

I have a God who loves me, and I am on his team.
He is all wise and powerful;
Jesus is his name.
Though everything is changeable, my God remains the same;
My God knows all that's happening, beginning to the end.
His presence is my comfort;
He is my dearest friend.

When trials come to weaken me, to bring my head down low, I call upon my mighty God.
Into his arms I go when circumstances threaten to rob me of my peace;
He draws me close unto his breast, where all my strivings cease.
And when my heart melts within me, and weakness takes control, he gathers me into his arms;
He soothes my heart and soul.
The great I Am is with me;
My life is in his hands.
The Son of the Lord is my hope;
It's in his strength I stand.
I refuse to be defeated;
My eyes are on my God.
He promised to be with me as through this life I trod;
I'm looking past all my circumstances to heaven's throne above.
My prayers have reached the heart of God;
I'm resting in his love.
I give God thanks in everything;

My eyes are on his face.
The battle is his;
The victory is mine.
He'll help me win the race.

Always put on the full armor of God. It will protect you from the attacks of the enemy. He is out to destroy you. Obey God's commandments—especially to love one another as he has loved us. Take an inventory of your heart and mind so that when you say that you love somebody, it is coming from the heart.

Do not make the mistake of having "hot lips and a cold heart." Treat people as you want to be treated—you will be better off. Pray to God each and every day for the guidance and correction of his Holy Spirit. There will be times in your life when you want to give up. Yield to the Scriptures of the Bible and have a little faith.

God will come into your life and move mountains that you would never believe he could move. All you have to do is be submissive to his will and watch him fulfill your needs. After you are with a church for so long, you will find out if they are in it to win it or are just going through the motions.

It is all about winning lost souls into the kingdom and praying for those who are still lost in the darkness so that they will come over into the light of Jesus Christ. I really love God, the Son, and the Holy Spirit with all my body, mind, soul, and heart. He knows this for sure. I am a living witness of his grace and mercy forever. I look forward to having everlasting life with him and through him. I look forward to sitting in heaven and praising him for what he has done for me.

My contact information is garyrisingstar@gmail.com

Printed in Great Britain
by Amazon